Dedicated to those with a wild imagination.

Introduction

This book aims to inspire creative thinking by prompting readers to visualize stories from imagined worlds or situations. Through the poems and accompanying illustrations, readers are invited to picture these stories in their minds and perhaps even extend the narratives beyond what is explicitly presented. The goal is for each poem to spark the the reader imagination and engagement, allowing them to explore and develop the stories independently.

CONTENTS

NATURE RECLAIMED

Nature Untouched - 9

Serene Blue - 11

Between Green Blades - 13

Above the Clouds - 15

Soil's Sentiment - 17

WONDERS OF WATER

The Blue Expanse - 21

Reef of Rainbows - 23

Forgotten - 25

Islands Apart - 27

Deep Black - 29

DREAD

Thinkers Fall - 33

The Room - 35

The Crawl - 37

Sleepless Leg - 39

Twisted Phantom - 41

INFINITE COSMOS

Among the Stars - 45

Contact - 47

Anomaly - 49

Dead Comet - 51

The Edge of Space - 53

TIMES BEYOND

Triton Tsunami - 57

The Blueprint - 59

Biometrics Invalid - 61

Amalgam ASHR - 63

Merciless Cloud - 65

Proto-Human - 67

CURIOSITY

NATURE RECLAIMED

Nature Untouched

Nature untouched,

With destinations untravelled,

See its secrets unravelled.

Free from intervention,

Unspoiled by man's invention.

Rivers blue,

Sunlight's serene refraction,

Nature un-squandered.

One would ponder

Upon this transcendent visage:

Could it thrive forever,

Untouched,

Yet met with curious fascination?

Serene Blue

This blue so clear,
The stream in the ear,
The bank sparkles bright,
Its rays reflect the light.

The serene blue deflects,
The stream flows and connects,
It moves steadily down,
With a continuous sound.

A crash that follows through,
The serene blue bellows too.

Between Green Blades

Unnoticed,

Small,

They roam

These beings not prone.

Their wings they flutter,

and with their beaks they chirp,

With their legs they scuttle.

Raindrops fall,

This is nature's call,

Between green blades.

Above the Clouds

Within this forest,
A giant stands grand,
Its roots spread far,
They spread wide.
Its branches are grand,

Its branches are its pride.
Above, above, above,
Higher, higher, higher,
To the canopy
Above the clouds.

Soil's Sentiment

From soil

It stands,

Undisturbed.

Petals unmatched,

Lush

Against the brush.

A focused eye,

An unrelenting gaze,

Towards the spherical blaze

A statement,

A soil's sentiment.

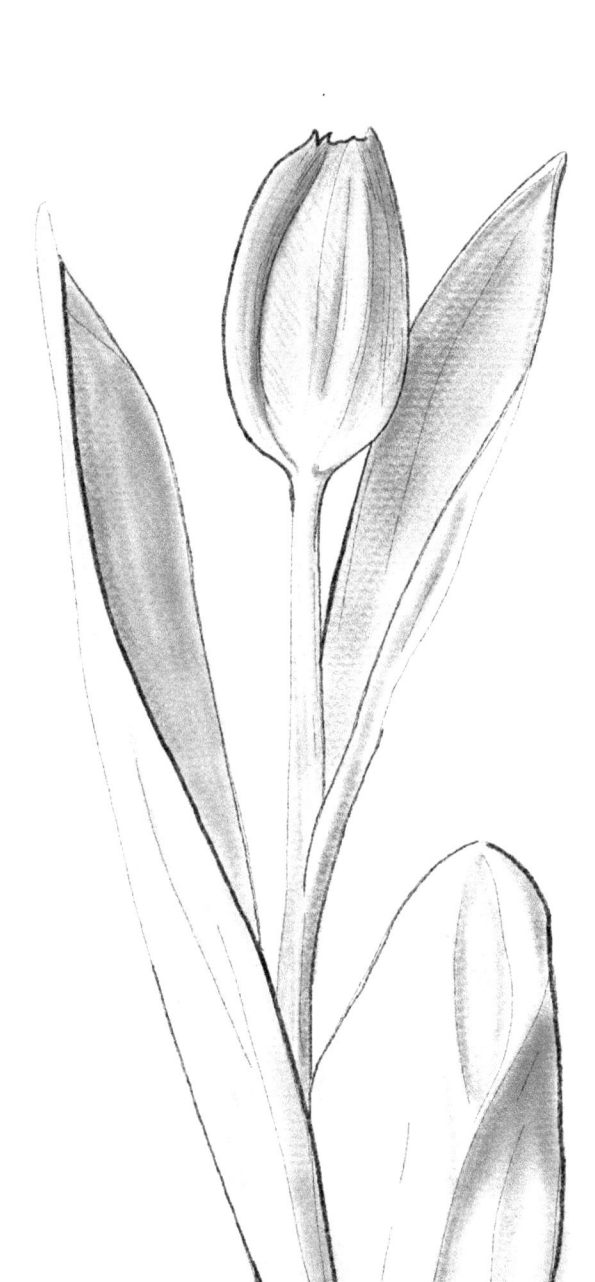

WONDERS of WATER

The Blue Expanse

This blue plain,

Can you see beyond?

Anything at all?

Past the blue expanse,

Beautiful,

As if in a trance.

Look above,

Look below,

Invert the sky,

Curious,

The expanse,

A blue trance.

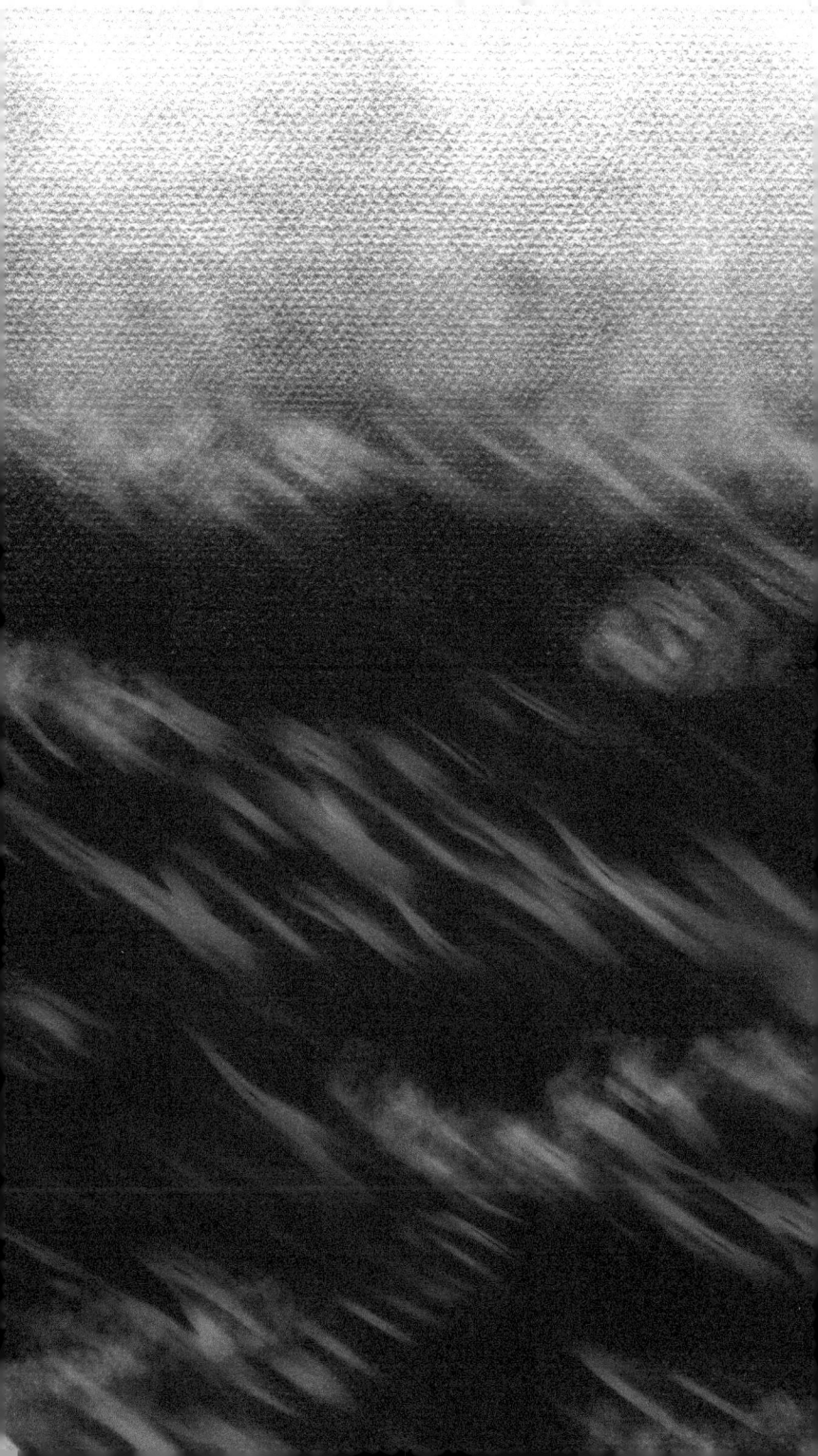

Reef of Rainbows

A multitude of colour,

A multitude of life,

They swim

Through crevices,

Through cracks.

They swim,

Blending with the colour,

Bending the light.

They live,

They swim.

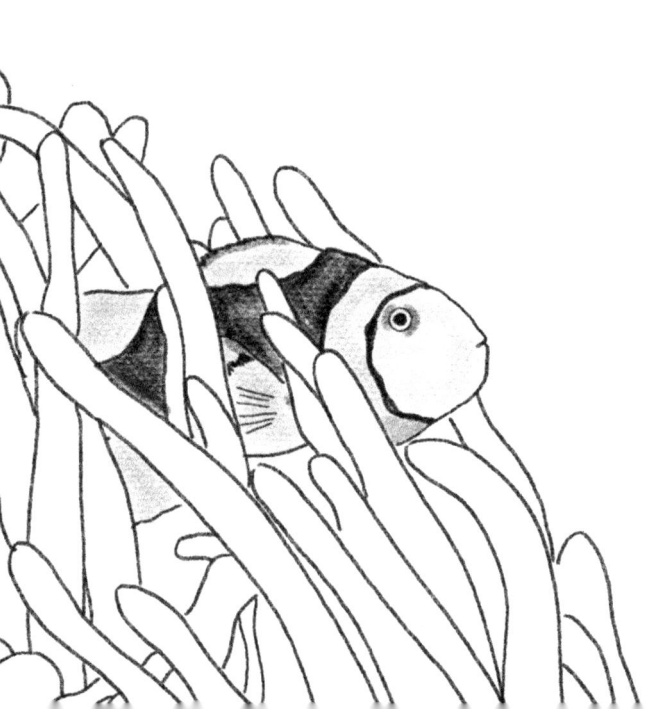

Forgotten

A structure,

Not belonging,

Lost to time,

A past divine.

New hosts remember

The old and dead.

Below it towers,

Once great powers,

Past forgotten.

Islands Apart

Faintly seen beneath,

Parallel,

They pierce.

The blue veil twists,

These small mountains,

Two rows sharp,

Islands apart.

Waves depart,

They sink,

They rise with monstrous foundation.

They clash,

The blue veil

A new jubilation.

Deep Black

This veil -

Black,

A cloak for monstrous minds,

A screech,

A roar,

Opening the minds door.

A maw?

A fabrication?

An imagined altercation?

Real?

These unseen beasts' next meal

Is death near?

Is this real fear?

Hallucinations?

You stop roaring,

But you continue to screech.

DREAD

Thinkers Fall

This thinker,

Thinks.

The past,

Time too fast,

Thinking,

And the mistakes amass,

As if an unrelenting flood,

A negative horde.

Strained,

The thinker points a finger,

What to blame?

Only one in the frame -

The past; it corrupts the present,

Future mind constructs.

To forgive,

To forget,

To suppress,

To confess.

The thinker

Detaches,

Like a flame it catches.

Mind consumed,

Never once resumed.

Now life consumed,

And life lost.

The Room

This room -

Where? Where? Where?

A place unknown,

An exit unshown.

Time, like the mind,

Glass -

Who? Who? Who?

Old, old, old,

Scold, scold, scold.

How? How, how?

OUT!

NOW! NOW! NOW!

Glass,

Glass,

Glass,

Don't forget

The past,

The past,

The past.

Forget now,

Forget the future.

The mind,

It breaks,

And there is

No exit.

The Crawl

So long,

The crawl,

So narrow.

The space,

So slow.

The pace.

Just enough room to crawl,

The pain

The ache

It all looks the same.

Pain and fear,

An escape not near.

Hours and days,

Hope lost,

Life is the cost

The toll,

The crawl.

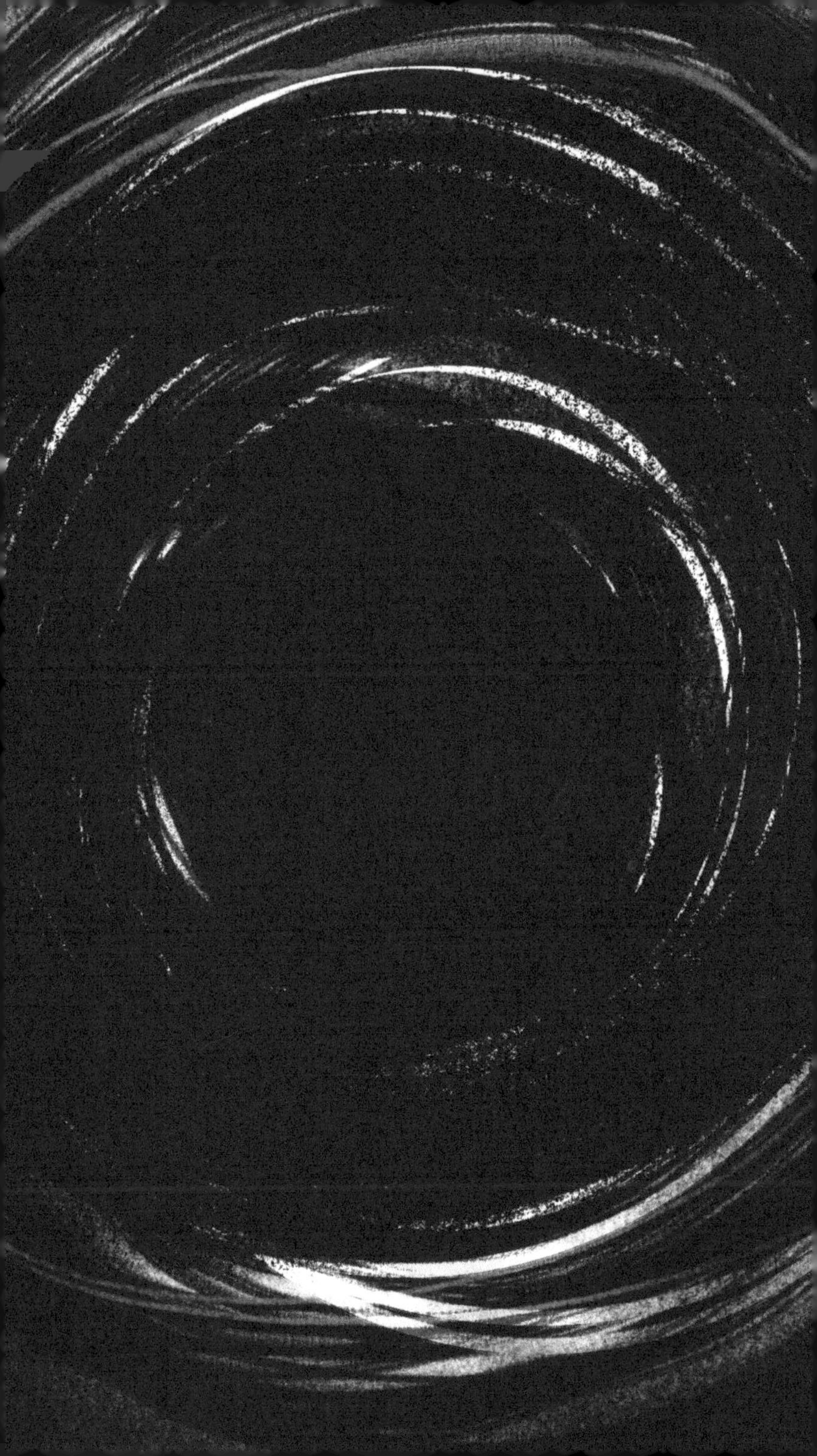

Sleepless Leg

This pond,

Long abandoned,

Forgotten,

At the bottom,

Not meant to be seen.

It rests,

You see it -

Long

Rough

But not a plant.

Then what?

It crosses the mind,

And fear you find.

Yet curious,

You want to bring

This unsettling thing.

Have you decided?

Have you confided?

Fear

Or

Curiosity?

Sleep,

In the night it creeps,

It keeps you awake.

Time passes and passes and passes,

Have you decided?

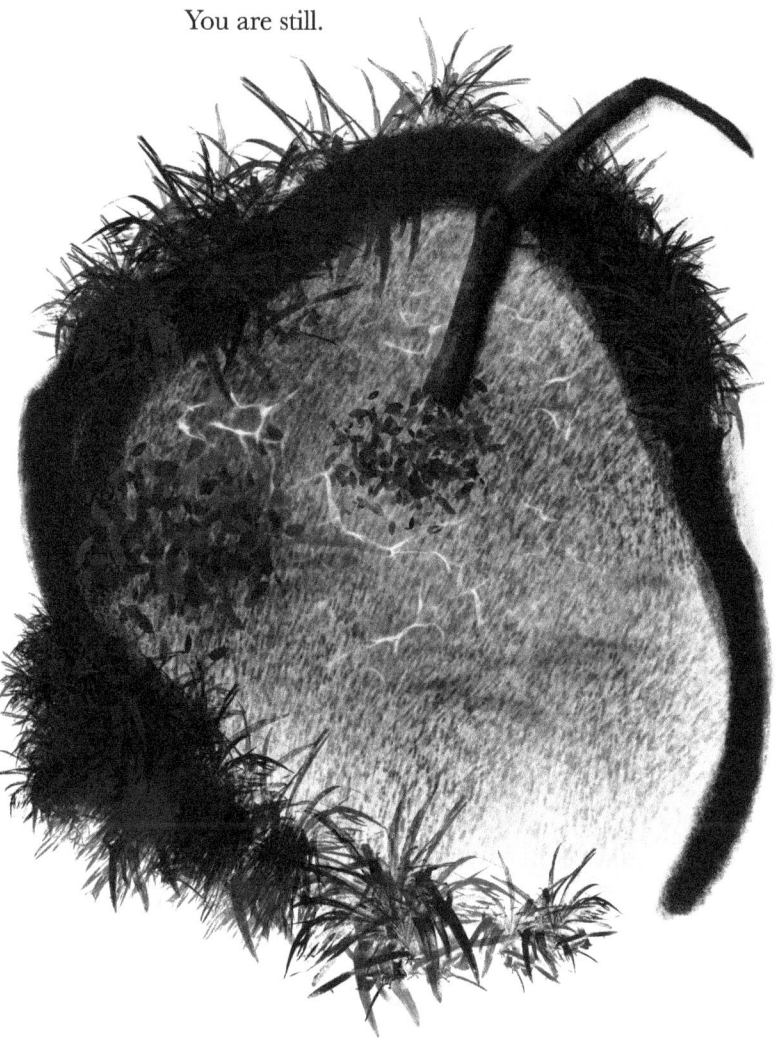

You are still.

Twisted Phantom

A bed,
Your bed,
It faces the door,
A hallway,
Long and dark.

You snore,
Suddenly you wake.
On edge,
You shake,
Heart rapid,
Offbeat.

You tug on your sheet,
A figure you see.
Eyes closed, terrified,
Petrified,
Wishing to flee.

Eyes open,
It is gone.
A sudden hoard
Of footsteps
And you hear
It is near.

Heart strained,
It stops,
Broken by fear.
Now,
Back to sleep,
Awake?
Not under the eye of the twisted phantom.

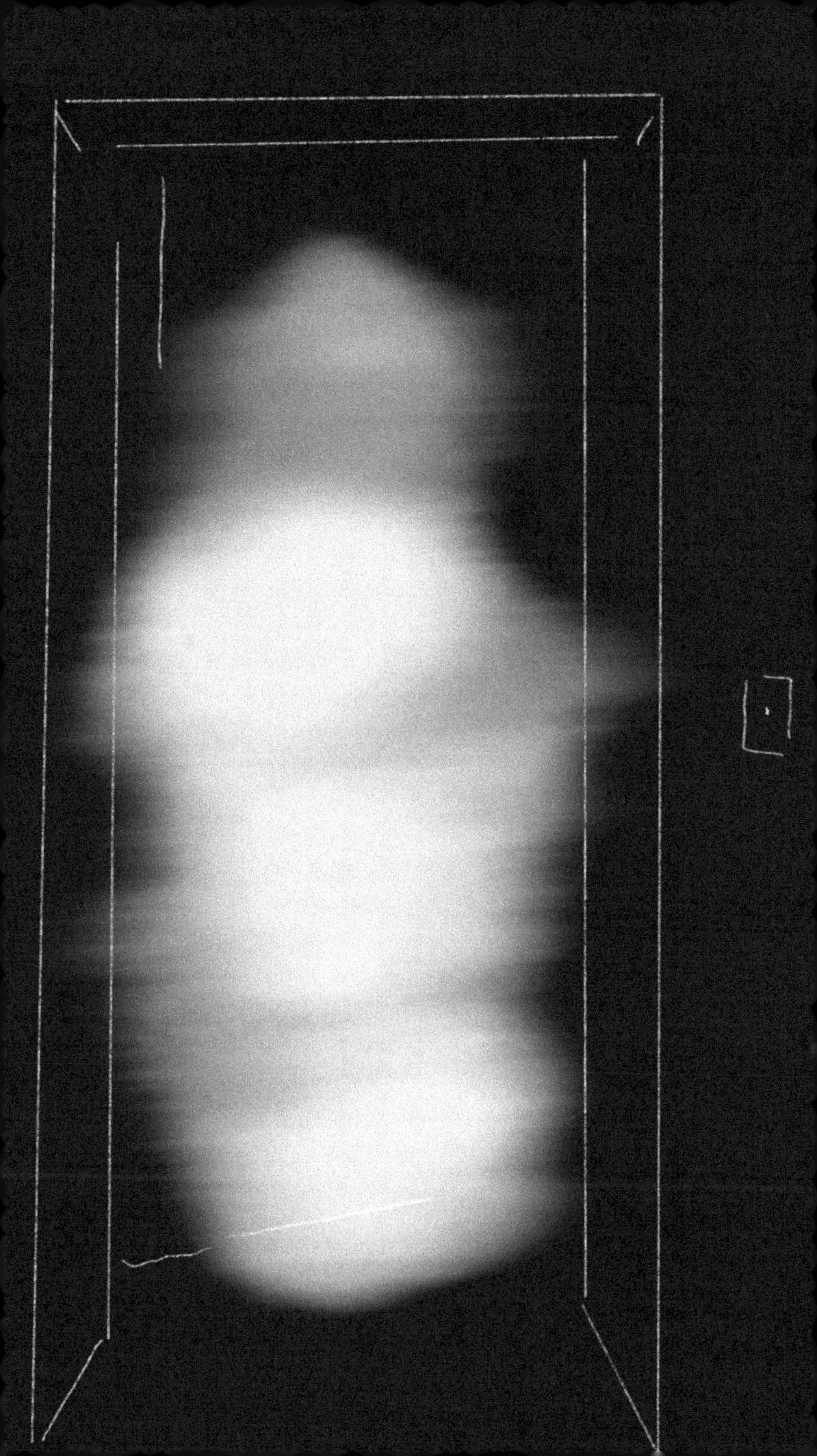

INFINITE COSMOS

Among the Stars

In space,

We travel,

We learn.

In space,

The human race

On an ark we call home.

We try to atone.

Together we travel,

Together we explore,

Together we survive,

Together we thrive,

Among the stars,

Not without scars.

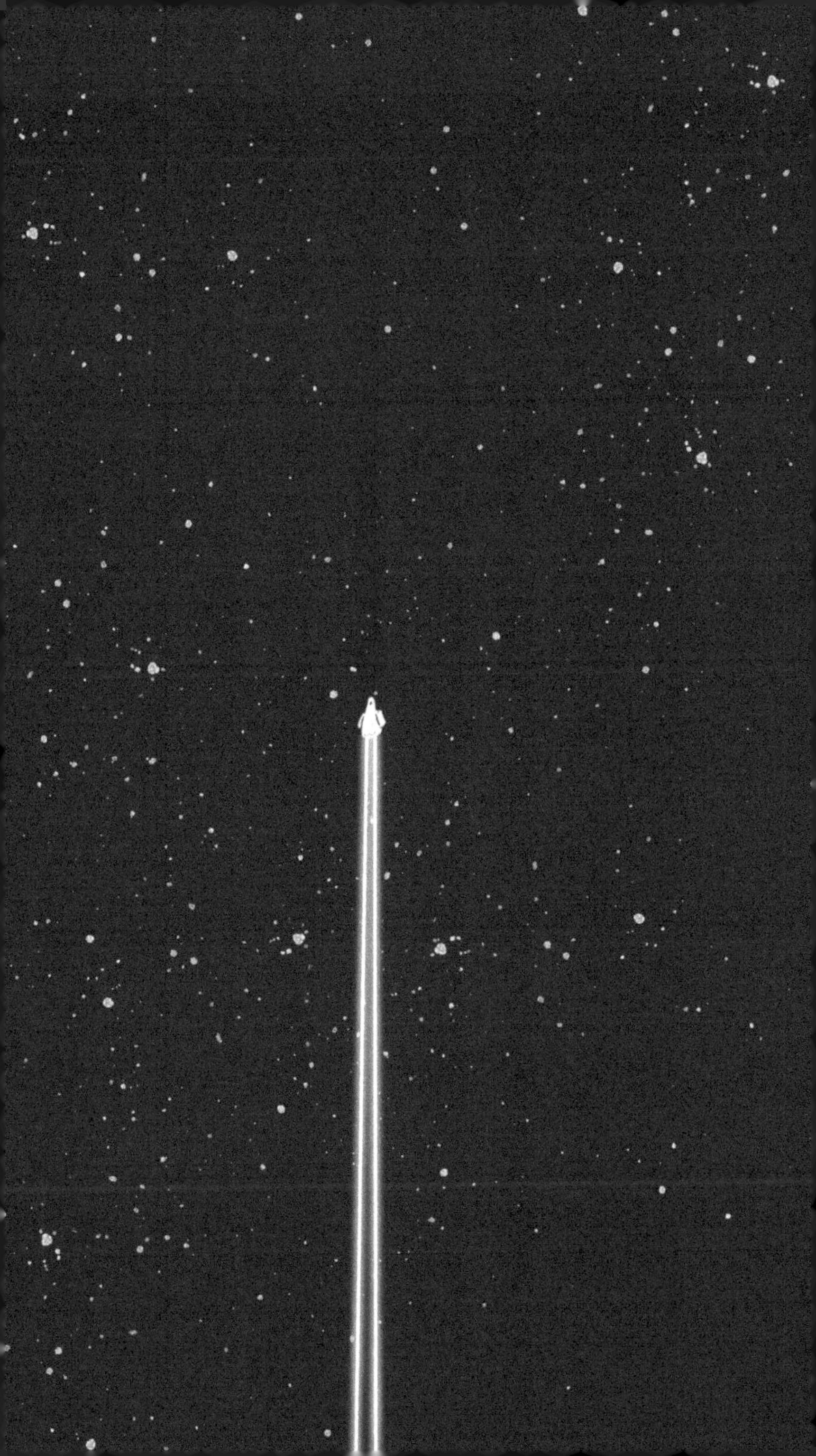

Contact

Like us,

They searched.

Like us,

They strived.

Like us, they survived.

And like us, they fled.

Their past?

How long did it last?

They tell us

Of a violent past

It was inevitable,

But it did not last.

And with time,

No longer us.

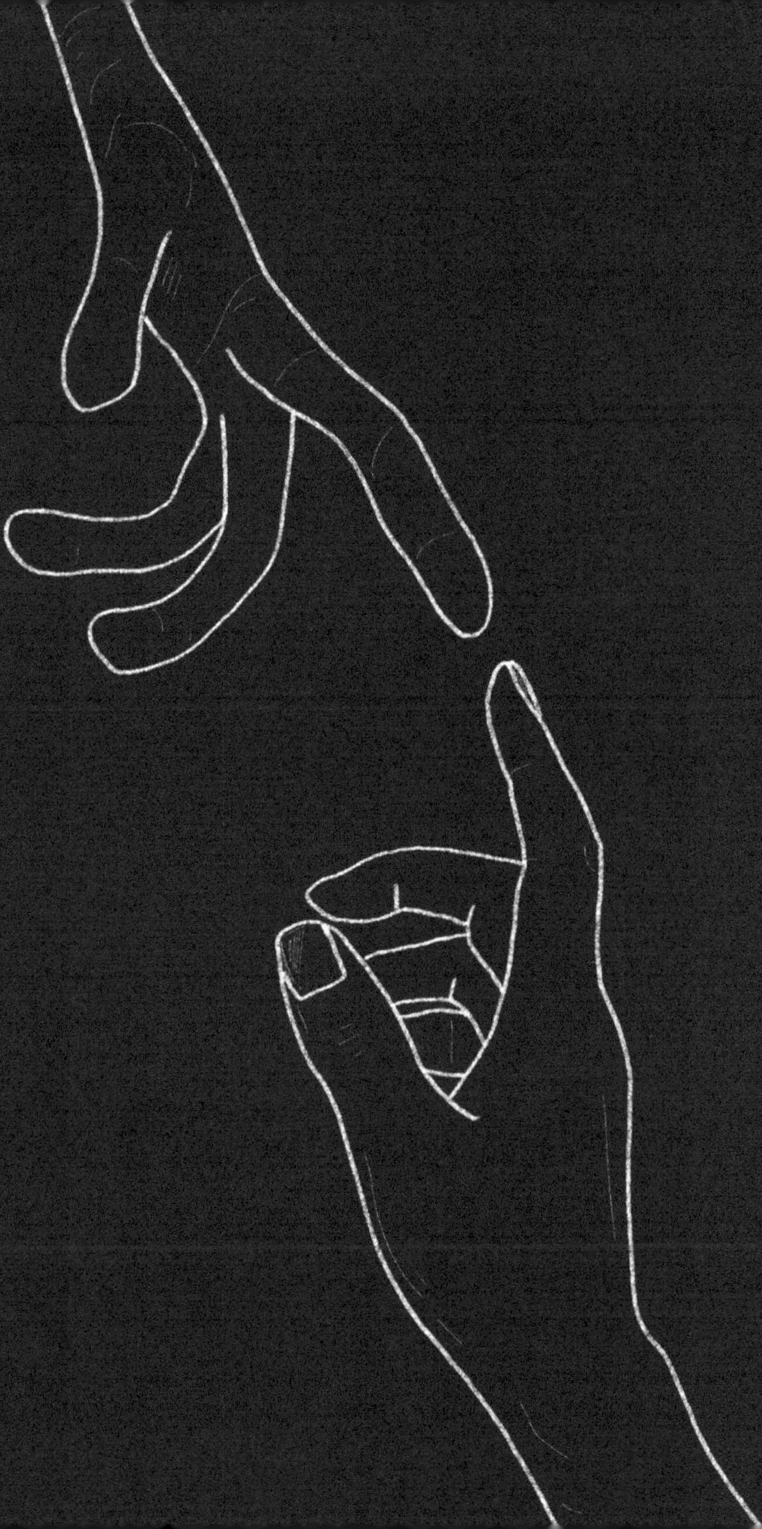

Anomaly

Through the Webb,
Is something seen?
Something illogical?

A planet,
Not enclosed
Strange,
Its core exposed.

Our laws ignored,
Our logic flawed?
An illusion?
A trick?

No,
Something real,
It steals our attention.

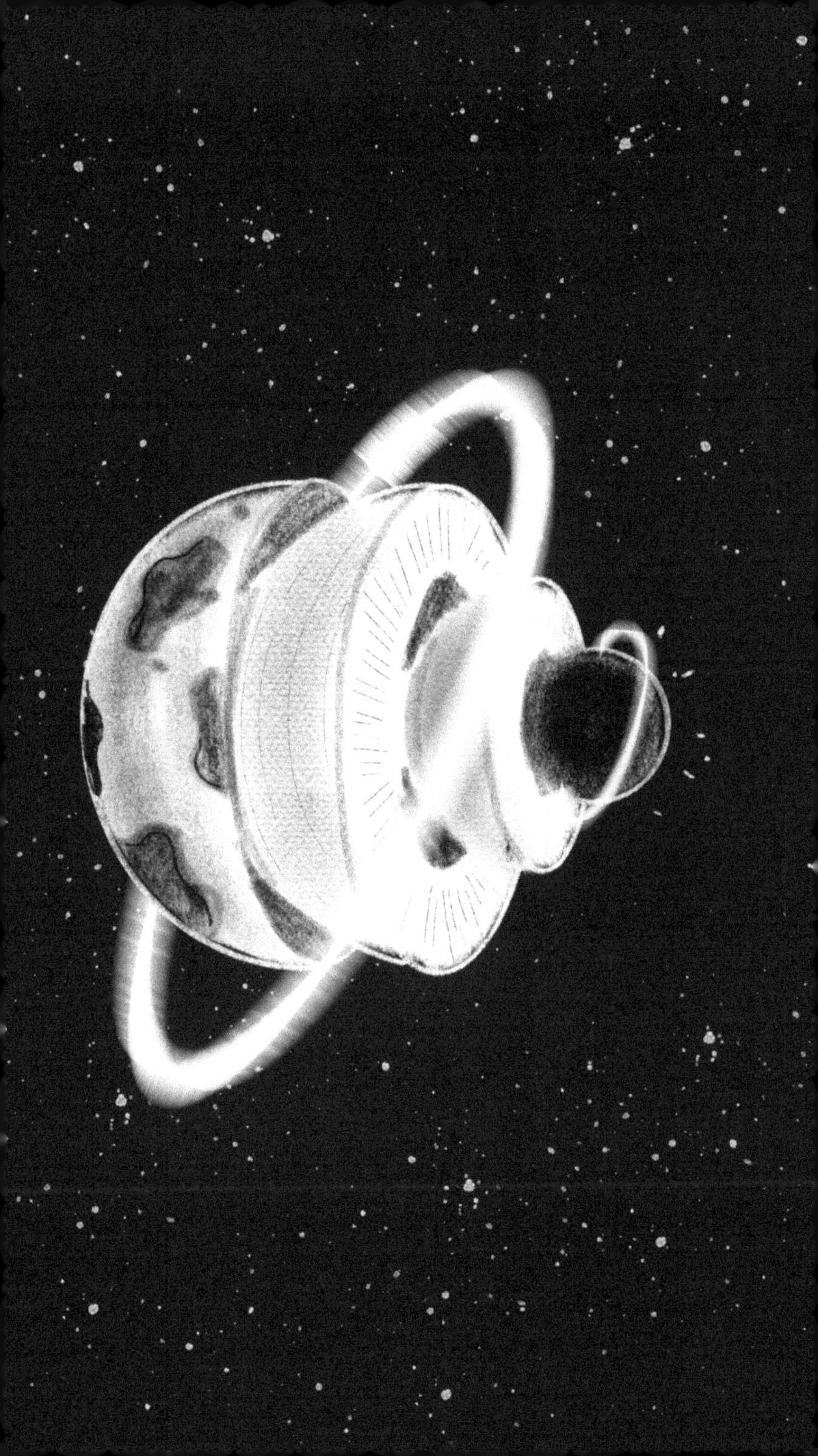

Dead Comet

Flesh-like,

Rotten,

From dead space,

Forgotten,

A horror unknown,

This strange mystery,

Alone.

For how long has it drifted?

It knows you're looking,

It moans,

It groans.

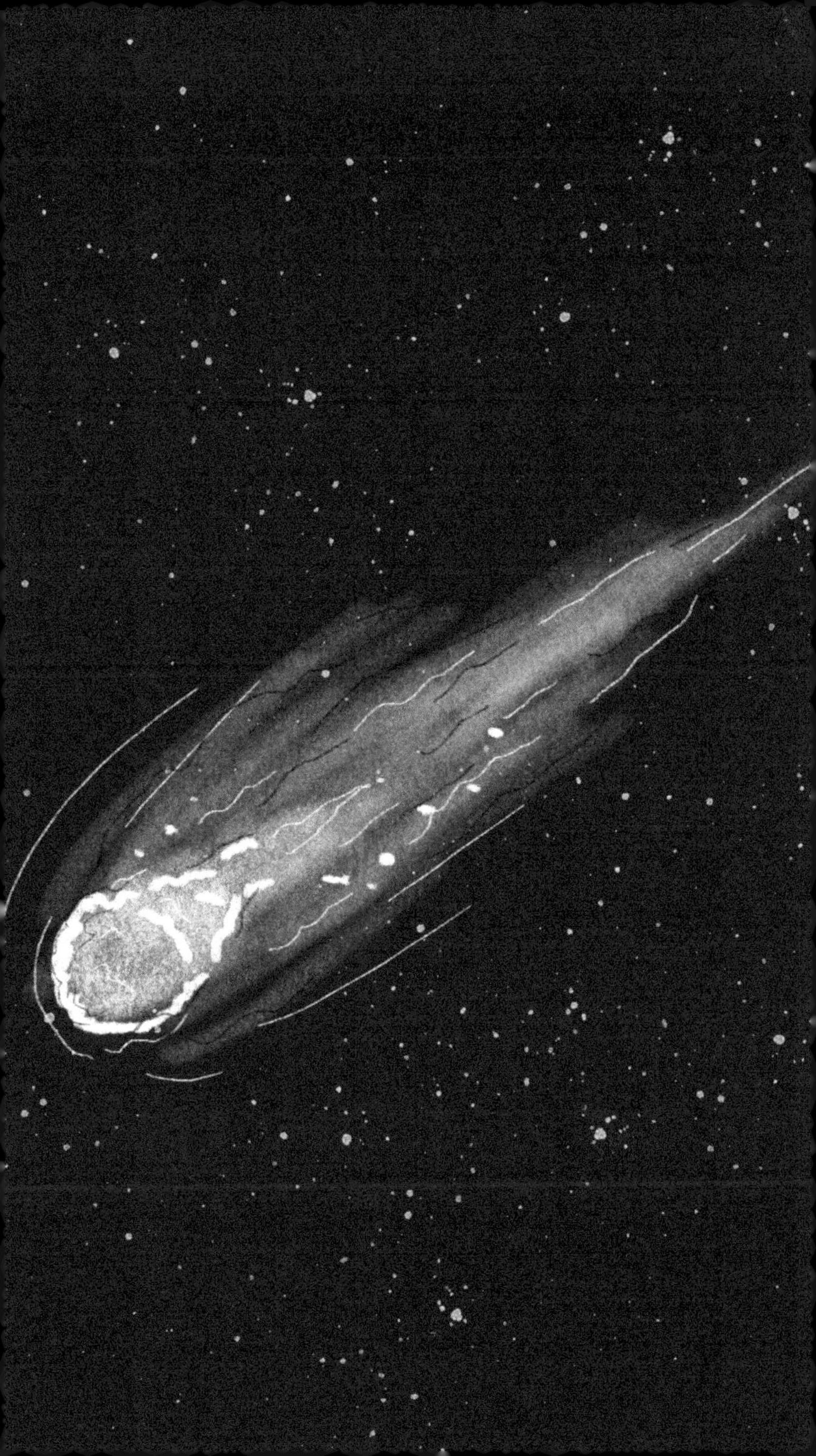

The Edge of Space

The edge,

An endless wall,

Endlessly tall.

A spectrum of colour,

Boundless reach

A living light,

A living dark,

The creator's spark.

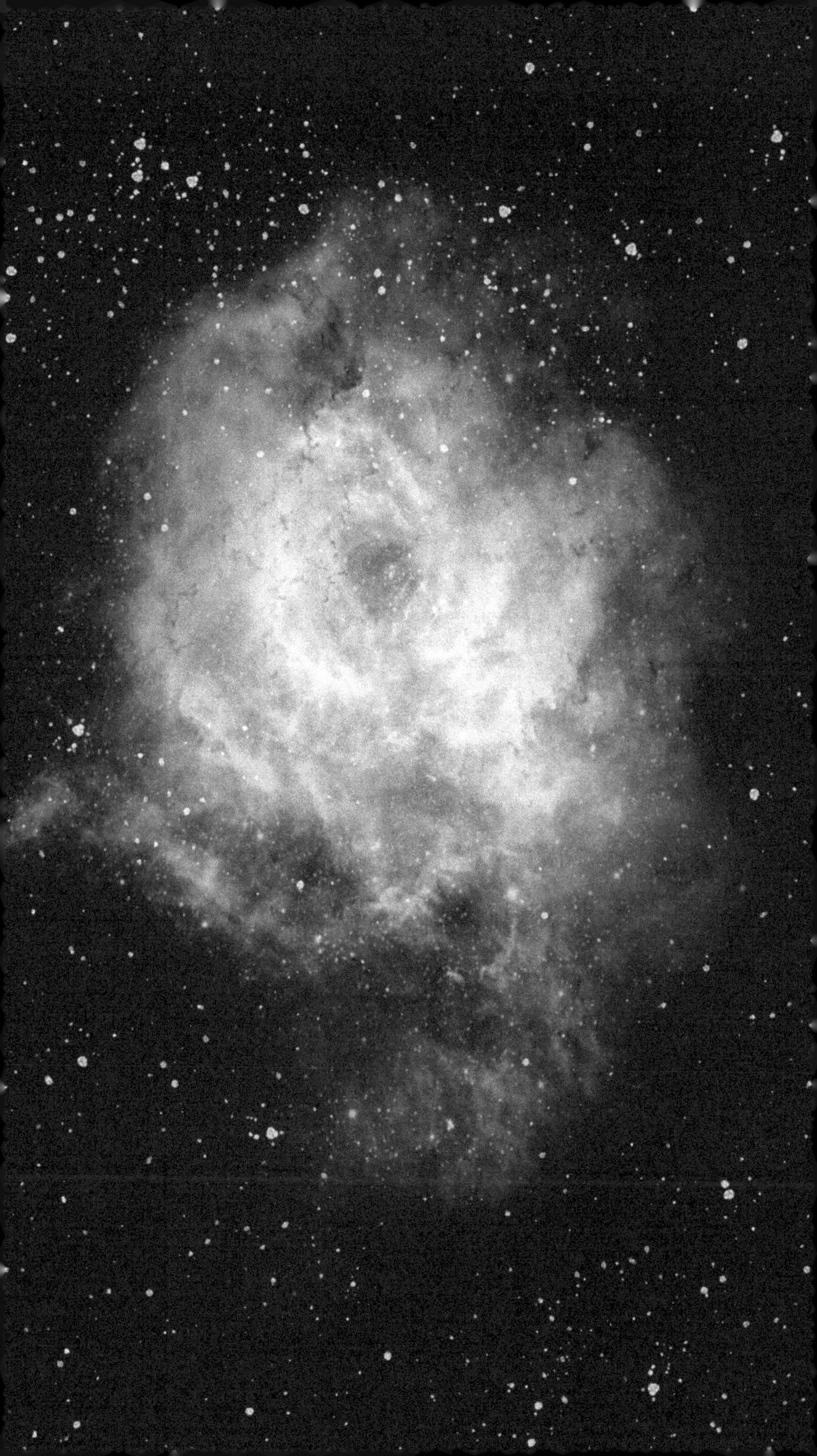

TIMES BEYOND

Triton Tsunami

Its design,

So sleek,

So smooth,

As if moulded by mercury.

Not driven by the meek,

Not driven by the mild -

It's the wild.

It glows,

Pulses,

Speed unmatched,

Like a bolt in the dark,

Gone in silence

The Triton Tsunami.

TSUNAMI
TRITON
TSUNAMI
TRITON
TSUNAMI
TRITON
TSUNAMI
TRITON

The Blueprint

In the wrong hands,
A threat to the world -
The power of the sun,
With terror,

The world it would shun,
Controlled by scum.

If developed,
This satellite,
The world
It would envelop.

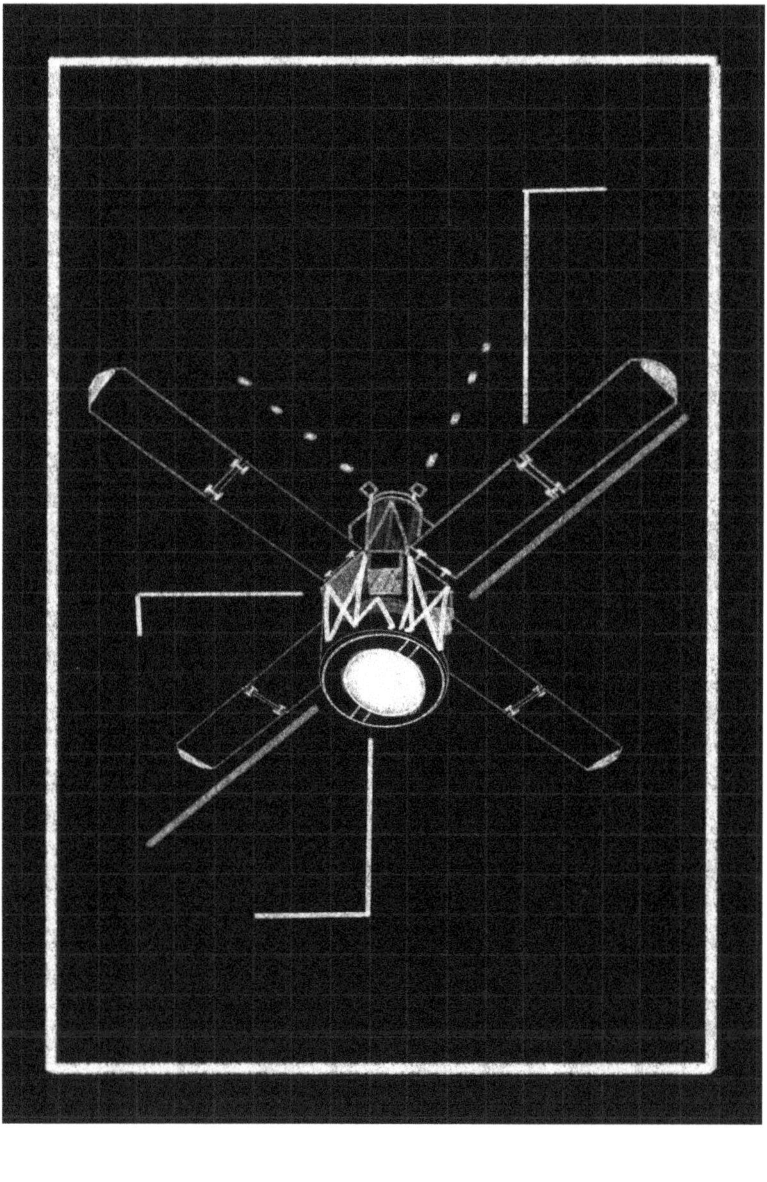

Biometrics Invalid

One fingerprint,

To open this door,

One fingerprint, nothing more.

To trick the scan -

A flawed plan.

'Fingerprint forged',

'Measures taken',

'Pain reaction ignored'.

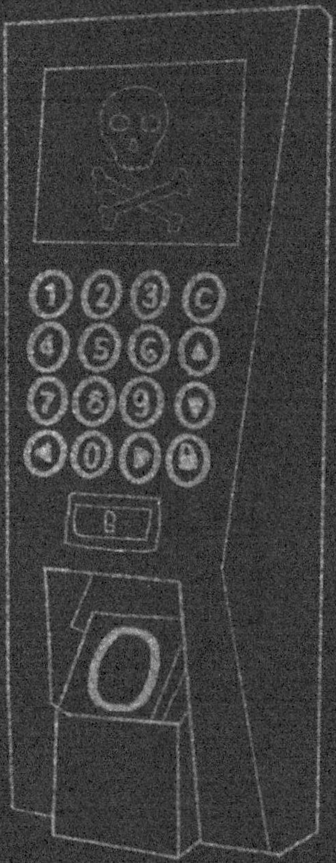
1 2 3 C
4 5 6
7 8 9
0

Amalgam ASHR

Amalgam's latest,

Versatility unmatched,

Distance?

The shortest,

The longest

Decimated.

One phase,

The amalgam shifts,

The battlefield rifts.

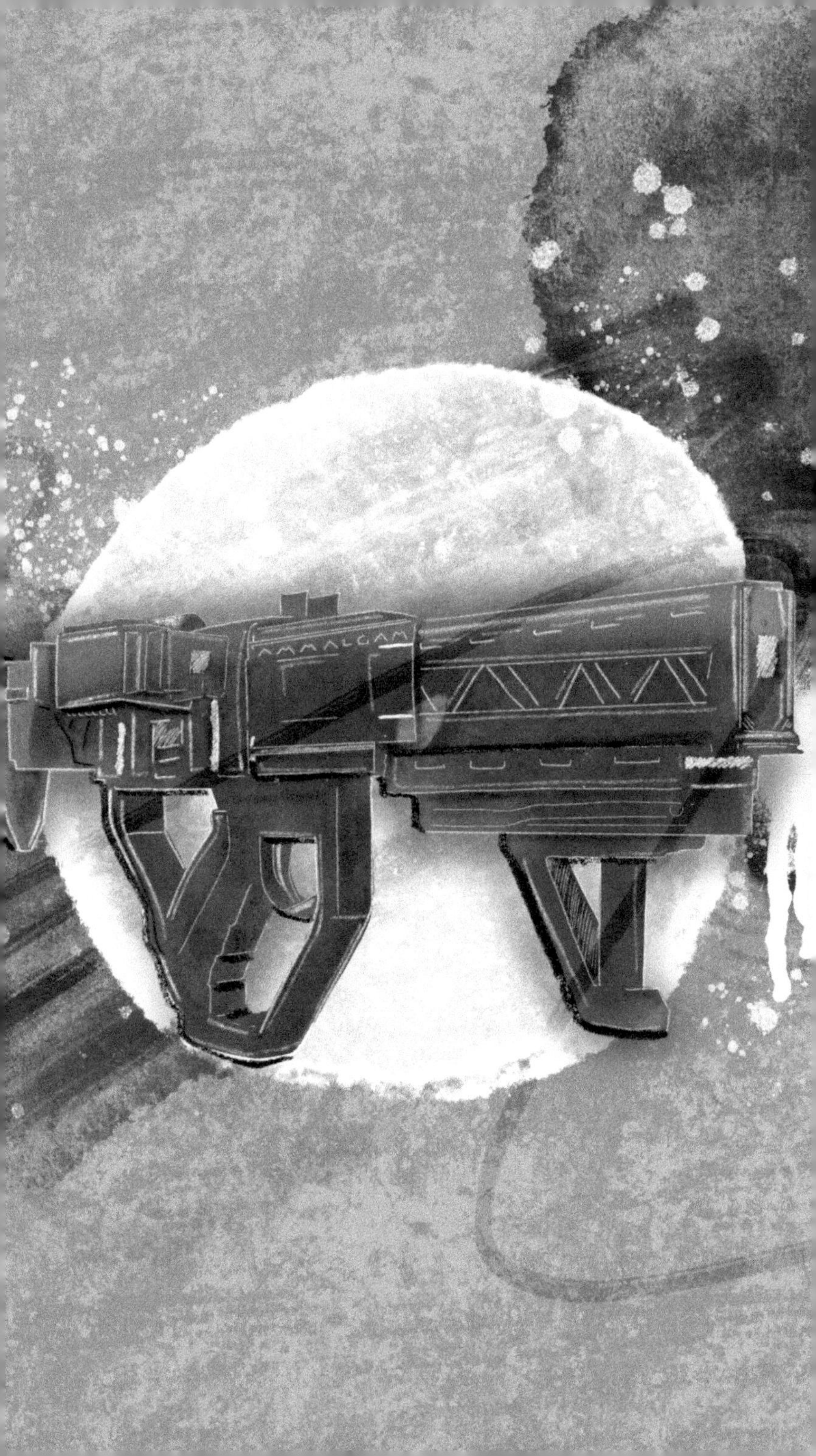
AMMALGAM

Merciless Cloud

A cloud without rain,

A machine of pain,

A drone,

A surveyor,

Omnipotent vision,

The world in fission

A man-made god.

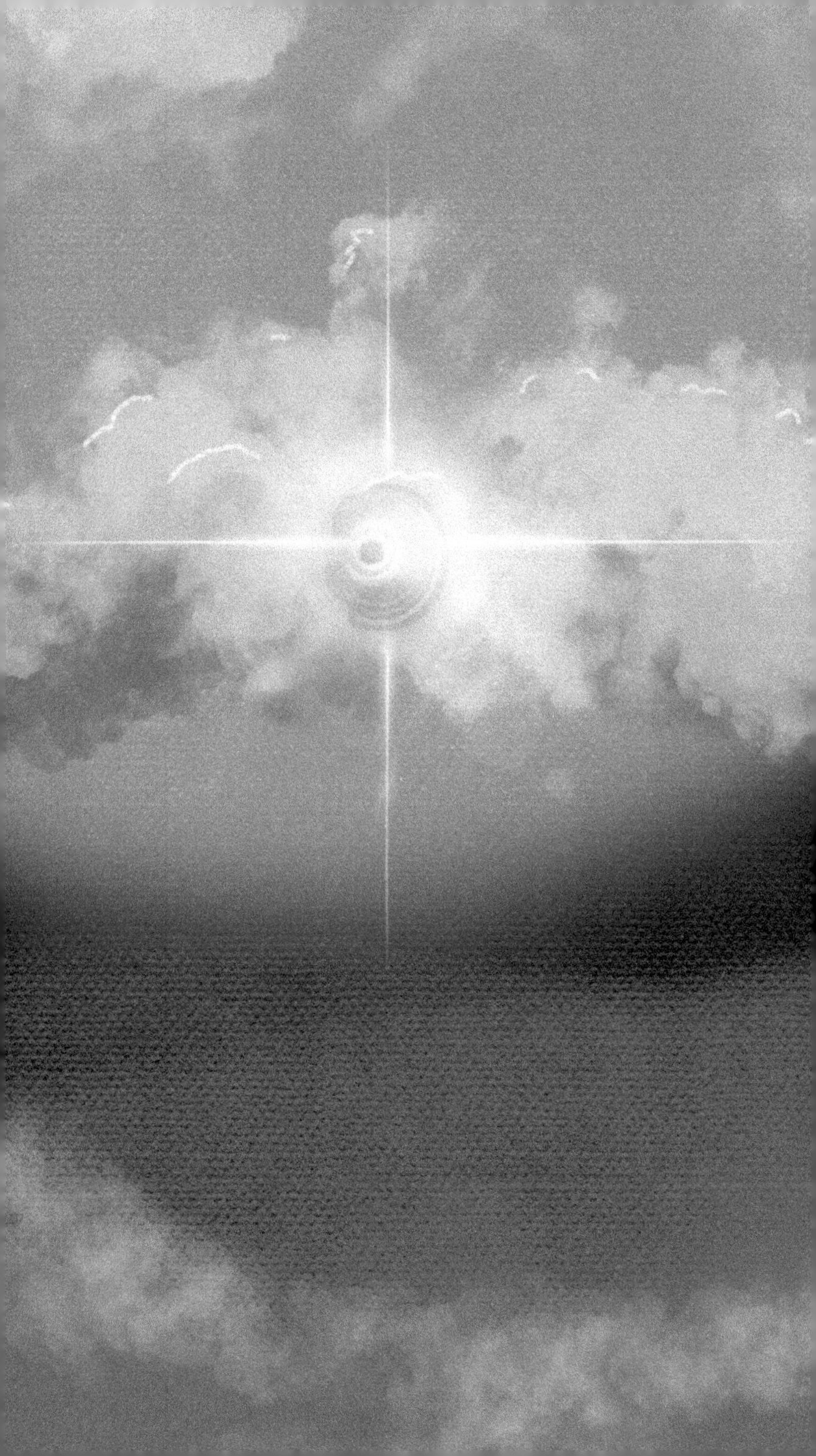

Proto-Human

Body inferior,
Body discarded,
The brain converted.

A new body,
Superior,
No longer inferior.

A body altered,
Feelings faltered,
Smarter,
Faster.

An improvement?
A body of metal,
Durable,
Humanity,
Lost, incurable.

Sam Vincent Butler is an emerging amateur poet from Birmingham. His debut collection, *Curiosity*, serves as a gateway to the imagination. Outside of his literary pursuits, Sam is actively involved with Thrive, a gardening charity where he nurtures both plants and community connections. Through *Curiosity* and his varied interests, Sam seeks to inspire and engage others, fostering a deeper appreciation for imaginative thinking and personal creativity.

Milton Keynes UK
Ingram Content Group UK Ltd.
UKHW051852281024
450367UK00019B/266